Wakefield Press

THE BRIDGE

Jelena Dinić arrived in Australia in 1993 during the collapse of Yugoslavia. She writes in Serbian and English. She is the recipient of the George Town Literary Exchange and The Arts Space residency in Rimbun Dahan, Malaysia, the Eleanor Dark Foundation Varuna Writers' Retreat in the Blue Mountains, and the Lighthouse Arts Hunter Residency.

Jelena's poems and short stories have been published in literary journals and anthologies, including *Australian Book Review, Australian Poetry Anthology, Australian Poetry Journal, Best Australian Poems, Jacaranda, Saltbush Review, Going Down Swinging, Westerly*, and the *Canberra Times*.

In the room with the she wolf, her first book of poems, was winner of the 2020 Adelaide Festival Premier's Unpublished Manuscript Award, and the Mary Gilmore Award for the best first book of poetry published in Australia in 2021.

Jelena lives in the Adelaide Hills with her family.

By the same author
In the room with the she wolf

THE BRIDGE

JELENA DINIĆ

Wakefield Press

Wakefield Press
16 Rose Street
Mile End
South Australia 5031
www.wakefieldpress.com.au

First published 2026

Copyright © Jelena Dinić, 2026

All rights reserved. This book is copyright. Apart from
any fair dealing for the purposes of private study, research,
criticism or review, as permitted under the Copyright Act,
no part may be reproduced without written permission.
Enquiries should be addressed to the publisher.

Cover design by Stacey Zass
Edited by Julia Beaven, Wakefield Press
Designed by Michael Deves, Wakefield Press
Typeset by Clinton Ellicott, Wakefield Press

ISBN 978 1 92338 856 7

 A catalogue record for this book is available from the National Library of Australia

 Wakefield Press thanks Coriole Vineyards for continued support

For Dimitrije and Katarina

'And as if carried somewhere else
there we stay'
'Nostalgia', Giuseppe Ungaretti

'From everything that man erects and builds in his urge
for living nothing is in my eyes better and more valuable
than bridges.'
Ivo Andrić, Nobel Laureate

Contents

At a door	ix
Displacement	1
The Process	3
Situation Y	4
On a Street Corner	6
Autumn Love in Four Parts	8
Unbuttoned	9
Dresses	10
The Red Dress	11
The White Dress	12
Shoes	13
A Quiet Crime	14
Unannounced	17
Wedding Guests	20
Choking on the Watermelon	21
George	22
Us and Other Guests	23
The Jetty	26
The Wall	27
Summer	29
Hope	30
The Rules of the Machine	31
Working with Carnations	33
Spring	35

Why?	36
Terribly Nice Things	38
Close Contacts	41
Knock, Knock on a Wooden Horse	42
The Box of Chocolates	44
The Telling of the Bells	46
At the River	48
Once in Paris	50
Royal Adelaide Hospital	51
Serbian Christmas	53
This Morning, a Fresh Beginning	54
Letting Go in Istanbul	55
Dying Art of Bargaining	57
Garden of Stones	62
Bridge of Sighs	66
Gumnuts	70
Acknowledgements	72

At a door
a heart knocks on both sides.
A handle threatens to shatter the world
at a most gentle turn.
There is nowhere I'd rather be.

Displacement

When I followed your voice
in a moment
mine was lost—
thinking
how after all this rain
I have no umbrellas left.

I forgot
my last umbrella on the bus seat
half-knowing
I would leave it there,
half-hoping I wouldn't.

I gave
the wrong destination to the bus driver,
who said this is your stop
even though it wasn't.
It was easier to leave
than to make him listen
to the language I didn't speak.

The rain sounded familiar.
I thought to ask
how you were doing
but I didn't—
the weather bored you,
you weren't worried about umbrellas,
where you went and why,
you spoke fluently
to me in the voice
I couldn't meet halfway.

I wished to speak better,
more clearly than the rain
which didn't make things easier
only amusing
when I lost all my umbrellas—
it was raining and I was running
towards my next stop,
to find
there was nothing left to lose,
only what couldn't be said.

The Process

How do you do it?
By doing things like this.

I thought it was only this,
not things like this.

Things like ...? Like this.
Not always. Similar.

Do you do this often?
That is what I do.

Why do you do it?
To undo what I've done.

Can you do that?
I can only try.

Where do you do it?
Here and there.

You have time for that?
That is all I have.

Situation Y

Yesterday feels like it didn't happen.
The voice in your head is a day louder.

Take small breaths.
In and out.

Pause.
This is just a panic attack.

Another thought can destroy you.
What you know turns against you.

A horse deserts you on a battlefield.
Before you learn why

shake the drawers open
search for the pen as if it were the proof.

When you leave things behind
they follow you.

It hurts like a mistake.
Yours or not, it is always yours.

Believe
you are believable.

This drawer needs reorganising.
A reminder you never needed.

Pull it out. Sort your debts.
Weigh your words.

Dip into this war.
Place a full stop near a wound.

On a Street Corner

When he asked for the money,
I asked for his name.
His eyes lit and opened wider.
A thin man and his city
two sides of the same thinning coin,
flipping roughly in between.
He walked his bike alongside me.
Jimmy, he said
offering his hand, smiling.
I felt the winter's day warmth.
It crossed my mind
to take his hand, change his luck.
Without asking,
I would give him a home.
A fireplace, a wild garden
and a few chubby children.
But I only had a coin.
He refused to leave me penniless,
said don't worry about it.
When I see him on the streets,
I am the one who wonders,
about coins, how they flip.

Their shine spent in dark pockets
for darker moments,
hoping
to light a way home.

Autumn Love in Four Parts

1.
Its last kick of colour.
The golden coins.

2.
A true you-make-me-happy yellow
before letting go. A gentle sway.

3.
A fall into abundance.
The lucky season.

4.
Every autumn turns to rust,
behind my back.

Unbuttoned

each

button

a

poem

in

your

fingertips.

Dresses

Sunbeams like blades play hit and miss
through the windows wide open.

A dazzle of daylight is all I own,
the silky turn of a season.

A few dresses hanging
in their worn-out tyranny.

A hello and goodbye
are spring decisions.

Daises will tell.
I trace disembodied presences,

the beaming patterns of first impressions,
imagined conversations.

Some real.
Often forgotten.

A few prints of the world left behind.
Lost translations once loved.

Loves me, loves me not.
Petals,

in a pocket full of hope
past its date.

The Red Dress

A cut of silk—
it fits into
a matchbox.

The White Dress

It lies on the bed,
as I sleep through all my alarms.

When I wear it, I pick my battles. Still,
I bleed, traditionally, unnecessarily.

On the floor the dress resembles
a sacrificed lamb,

the shell of a body stabbed in the back
But inside,

it is gentle like glass,
decorated with fingerprints.

Occasionally, I step out
free as an arrow,

or a wild stag
with antlers reaching for the sun,

dreaming of pebbles
on top of the rocks

high in the mountains
rising with the dawn.

Guiding the light in.

Shoes

Stabbing forward, loud and furious!
You think you will reach the stars?

You have nails in your belly.
Pain is meant to fit.

Your skin shines
like a patent headstone.

You step on your earthly promises,
there will be no wedding.

The world left behind
is our new beginning.

Come.

I push my foot into your throat.
Watch where you go.

A Quiet Crime

1.
She visits my dream
quiet and foreign
the only blonde in the family.
Poetry stitched
in her petticoat
a gift from a German soldier.
I want to ask
how far did you go?
All the way
to the river?
Just once,
drowning your wedding band?
In the mirror
I search for the clues.
She comes and goes
through the glass
as she pleases.

2.
Who is to blame?
Her wall stain repainted
white over red
again, and again.
Not true some say—
No blood was spilt.
They saw her in Austria
or was it Hungary
the dressmaker
flirting with floral
silk and batik around her neck.
Husband denies the knots.
Cuts the tangles in her name.

3.
I write to forget
my snakes
crawling out,
nature's venom
in the ballad retold.
A different poem
in my chemise.
With a street etiquette
I walk
fine lines,
a cross-stitch
pattern of life.
Less champagne
more brandy—
a drop to the ground,
a river turns
towards a lake,
an unbuttoned dress
in my hands
confessing.

Unannounced

1.
I move through life—
sometimes backwards,

often softly,
against the breeze

toward a place
where travel ends

and I land
in time to unpack.

2.
Today,
the linden trees are sawn from their roots,
the siskins look for new branches.
Far away a couple become a thought.
I walk the streets between here and there
deep in moonlight, the silence
noble, the night turning back time.
I don't mind being lost,
or late home,
the moon is behind me,

behind the clouds
that move across the street.
Suddenly
'hello'
in passing by
and a 'good to see you'
over the shoulder
feels warm,
like a small sigh
in a summer dream.

3.
When I enter the house,
I turn the lights on in every room.

Let the neighbours see the house come alive.

I open the wardrobe, the photo album,
try an old dress, rinse the wine glasses.

I am sixteen again. The mirror is grey.
Its face distorted with each of my returns.

In the dark
the lamp shines a light on new rules.

Both of us try to play nicely.

4.
Next to the mirror an old umbrella.
It opens like a heart to a friend.

I hold it firmly to my ribs
and walk under its blackness,

careful not to fall deep into myself,
into the memories,

voluminous and shaky,
avoiding the rat holes that sucked in the years,

yearning for the joy
that slipped through my fingers,

and to protect what's left
I am repeating the words

stay away from my rain

without making a sound.
I fall on my bed

with the heaviness of a beast
that has lost a few lives

and end the play fight
with a long howl into the night.

Wedding Guests

A set of cake plates and wedding rings
are marked-down memories,
but Romani girls dance to church bells,
as if a marriage will last forever.

All wedding songs belong to them.
On their wrists
charm bracelets keep time.
From their ears
red cherries swing like chandeliers.

One, looking at the bride, says:
'*Ti si lepa*'—you are beautiful.
She is tiny, fits into the eye.
She asks for money, but the guests pretend
they have none.

She says, 'You have; you have!'
And runs away laughing, laughing.
Dancing, singing, cursing.
Knowing.

Choking on the Watermelon

In summer's shadow,
under the walnut tree
we were not allowed to laugh
when we ate the watermelon.
Our father cut it open,
each slice sailed
from his hands into ours,
bursting cold.
Our lips trembled at some funny thought,
unspoken, infectious.
'Don't laugh,' he said. Again.
We held our breaths innocently,
like baby snakes in the grass, playing.
We spat the seeds between our feet,
beetles waiting for us to die laughing.
When my father lifted his hand in the air,
the wasps circled our watermelon faces,
our sticky hair, hands and feet.
Our daredevil giggles were turned into glue.
Tender bites of childhood
went down the wrong way,
in laughter, toward the dirt
like a life-sweet offering,
the future forevermore
with a faint scent of death.

George

From a café on Halifax Street

The world dazzles at the edge of a street.
People in a café juggle the morning take-aways.
George places a branch under a wobbly table. Then
warms his hands around a mug,
as if warming a quiet thought.
A wave of sunlight splashes over those
who hurry to be someplace else.
George is not in a hurry.
He has already been here and there,
often in the company of a friend.
This morning, a ladybird lands on his sleeve.
Her tender wings gift-wrapped in sunbeams.
George turns to an empty chair. He smiles,
holding close small miracles, like coffee and friends,
the evenness in his world, the thought that
who can't be seen is not really missing.

Us and Other Guests

For Jacqui Boylan

1.
The world slaps you as it turns away
and you arrive at a Welcome sign:

Refugees, this way.

You carry your land on your shoulders.
In front of you is an upside-down way.

2.
When Nepali fathers meet each other they ask:
Which refugee camp are you from?

Some letters are missing in Dari.
Others unspoken in Burundi.

No 'look me in the eye' in Burmese.
All mothers cry at night.

Diverse streams of this one world
like letters in the alphabet,

azbuka, or sa ka lone.
The flight of a language.

From left to right
the ink will spill.

Each word needs its letter.
Each letter, its alphabet.

Two hands signing—
fingers full of sunlight

sifting the words through their net.
Which do we keep?

A kiss,
a hug, a hello.

A cup of tea and a warm dish.
We are all each other's guests.

3.
I take my father to a doctor.
I justify his presence. He shrugs.

In our house I say the final word.
In English.

The person on the phone tells me
to tell my parents

life is easier with a Google account.
Even children know that.

4.
The children inside us,
around us, those still to come.

They grow, learn, play,
sometimes they don't.

The Jetty

For Kate Llewellyn AO

The sea was our looking glass—bewitching, inviting.
Our footsteps disappearing in the sand. That day,

we saw the fishermen return to the quiet of their catch.
Their fish slipped away like our precious moments.

What are you waiting for? you asked,
leaning against the rails on the jetty. I leaned closer,

felt the pulse of a poem. From the wilds of my mind
all my hooks cast out for your salt-flavoured words.

Often, there was a catch—and a few well-worn excuses:
the laundry, the babies, a warm dinner on the table.

As we spoke, the winter chill tinged our cheeks coral
and perhaps, from the sea depths of your eyes,

I saw all my poems surfacing, eager and
delicate like paper boats in the waves.

You looked ahead, believing, trusting,
when I let them drift towards the high seas.

The Wall

Once upon the time in Dubrovnik

1.
I walk the seawall.
Here, it is easy to fall
for the charm of a stone—
smooth and glistening.
Leaning over is foolish
like that crab in the sea
thinking sideways
as if she could crack open her shell,
and climb out of her rocky life.

Then?
Nothing
is promised although
young men throw coins
into Onofrio's Fountain
believing otherwise.
They drink from the mouths
of the sixteen maskerons—
their lips wet with luck.

Further up the unnamed street
toward the tower with no doors
my balcony clutches the wall

like a stone mollusk
waiting for high tide.

2.
The view drapes itself
with the old habit of a summer night.

Someone says it's nice to see you
as I look for what I remember.

Two little boats sail away.
What is lost the sea brings back,

only saltier.

Two chairs on the nearby balcony
are arranged like signs of life

or even love inside the walls.
Washed sheets in the wind

mirror the birds flying, or
is that just a dream pegged back?

My suitcase is full of excuses.
Expensive returns.

The sea unsettled in blue,
lifts slowly toward the sky.

Already I have overstayed.

Summer

The sand turns into a pebble,
a heart into stone.

The summer reminds me of a swim after sex
then blows its festive whistle and dies a lazy death.

Our dream-life boat
is sinking into the bed of corals.

We are two specks in the sea
fighting for breath like fish in small nets.

We are breathing through the hourglass.
The sand is slipping down our throats.

Some seas cannot be crossed.
We forget why.

Hope

There is always hope,
but what we hope for
changes.
We hope to live well
then, we hope to die well.

The Rules of the Machine

Through the back door
I am smooth as a thief.
Machines pose like beasts
yet I hear them squeak
under the belts and chains
as if a soul
is breaking inside.

The air is compressed.
With friction
the temperature rises.
I feel the fabricated heat.
The gradual revolution forbids
touching the parts
in operation
but in the down corner
my force is my instinct.
I lean,
lightly tap my mouth to machine.
I am
taking, gulping.

A stroke of sunlight
on the machine's lustre finish,
captures me tipsy.
I wipe my mouth with a sleeve
as if
wiping away the bitterness
is possible.

Working with Carnations

'We all know the way,'
says George. 'Sometimes,
it is a slow drive.'

In my lap the flower of mothers
'a perpetual carnation'
buds wired to the styrofoam heart.

George says,
'We are almost there.'
Around the corner,

stones raise their heads.
At the wide-open gate
we give way to those before us,

then drive slower into
the inner neighbourhood of life.
Always next door

to the homes of the beloved.
Here lived ... Here died ...
A careful step to the edge of a grave.

I fear falling in, still peek
inside the Earth's mouth.
It's staring back at me—

persistent and dark.
A reminder of a photograph,
the one we have all taken

travelling in life,
wearing a holiday smile,
singlet and thongs, staring

into the oblivion of a lens
that captures us closer.
We rinse our hands

in water with petals
excusing their emptiness.
Only flowers will quietly

slide down the dirt's throat.
One day we may find them
blossoming again.

Spring

September in Australia, 2022

Today,
I promise not to cheat
myself to happiness.
Or stumble when
walking out.
The impossible
will pass.
This spring.
The rain.
Beyond the window,
a bird takes its earthworm,
flies away.
A day at a time,
the leaves will grow
and the spring is no more.
That is all.

Why?

We shared a cigarette
in front of the grammar school.
Small shots of smoke traced us

over the winter's icy glow.
Light was a blur far behind.
The snow was not white.

People walked past us.
Never saw us.
Their eyelids heavy with uncertainties.

Our borders closed in on us
or were we just growing closer?
Sometimes, the fear decided.

Under an old coat
we counted the ribs on our bodies—
in a panic, tickled each other away.

Our laughter was escaping
like a separate entity.
I arrived without it.

My words sound foreign now.
I unpack and inhale a breath of spring,
and everything, eventually, is just lightness.

A puff of a question in a distance—why?
My multiple interpretations of it,
reduced meanings, disconnected dots

until there was nothing left
to say, or hold back,
hands free of touch.

I don't return for a while
but when I do
I hear clearly

words scraping between my ribs:
If you only knew
you would never have left.

Terribly Nice Things

1.
In the afternoon sun
his back is a golden leaf of skin.

I spread my fingers on it
let him guess what I want.

A few nice words, and
I watch his shoulder blades

squeeze out their meaning.
My fingers move

as if fingerprinting a leaflet,
covering the old writing.

I softly push him over the line,
a little closer to our future.

A scar for a scar
is a tailored approach.

A love play unbuttoned.
His mouth on my neck.

I smile. He knows.
Where we end, we begin.

2.
Walk down slowly,
loveliness.
Is this our street?
Watch your step.
It is November.
The long line of jacarandas
throw their petals your way.
Don't think of snow.
Here is the downfall
for other reasons.
On this side of the world
we turn to each other
and away
like two sides of November
and every street leads to us.

3.

No one enters the page
with a heart on the line.

An analogy snaps in half,
no sound from the wounded.

This is as close as
we can get to love.

There will be other poems.
Altered. Repaired.

Some will not tell.
Forgive them.

Forget them.

Close Contacts

My husband has returned. A traveller
whose flight was cancelled has found his way home.

He slowly unpacks
while I make space for the unexpected.

The house is full of him. I find him everywhere.
He hovers in the kitchen and takes over the knives.

He lifts paper to the window's light,
slices it with the sharpest blade.

I keep saying wash your hands, this virus is deadly.
We wait from a distance for the world to return.

We crossed the list of our commitments.
He cuts the tender loins and offers a slowly cooked dinner.

I look for a tablecloth.
We talk and take time to hear how each other's sentences end.

The sky is empty of temptation. In the corner,
the suitcase still lurks with a broken zip

and an old address. An invitation.
If we had a choice, where would we rather be?

Knock, Knock on a Wooden Horse

> 'Do as you like with me. I'm your parcel. I have only our
> address on me. Open me, or readdress me.'
> Ted Hughes, *Birthday Letters*

1.
I find the frilly snippets concealed in stripes.
The shiny paper. Its contagious pink prettiness.
All I think about is how to keep it.
Ribbons rifting from their knots. Their silky
offerings of terror, accidently perfect.
Their edges curling tongues. Cut them off.
Unwrap. Find a way to say I can't give it back.

2.
Which is the language of giving? Lavish French?
Was the biggest gift in history the Statue of Liberty?
The love of freedom? Taj Mahal was a gift. Two lovers
lying in marble. The luxury of the fearless.

3.
A poem ago, a gift was lightness,
the rustling sheet of paper in my hands.
The noise, a soft weight of meaning.
A gentle hold. It was almost enough.
I will miss pretending it is mine.
I can still hear the screeching
of another name written all over it.
Give it back. Let go.
Someone else is waiting for it.

The Box of Chocolates

They were a birthday gift.
Or a replacement for it.
As a child I watched them on a shelf.
My mother said no.
When you gave them to me
I thought of women born hungry.
Small explosions of pepper notes
the coated fruit inside my mouth
a guilt-centred bite.

When I opened the box
the life inside me
was wrapped in your life,
other lives coiled close.
I couldn't tell what would happen next.
I just had one. Or two.
Then the rest.
I took them with rum and cream.
A tickle grew inside me
like a serpent thirsty for milk.

Each was meant to be the last.
The luxury I couldn't resist.
I licked the sweetness like an addict,
called your name for more.

You spoke new English words,
I tasted their assorted meanings.
Or bit my lip, bittersweet.
A blood orange on my tongue.

From my mouth to yours.
Hard-boiled treats for armed forces.
My head fell into your lap.
For a moment you loved us both.

The Telling of the Bells

The sound of the bells on Flinders Street.

The inside of their mouths is beaten.
They will not tell for whom they sway from side to side.

Two half-bloomed flowers like sudden lovers,
hanging for dear life.

Their dangling tongues.
How easily they reach the highest note.

One minute to midday and the bells' song
will rise like a promise,

freed from their iron hearts. Listen for
its subtle curl down the rooftops

fitting tightly with the day's routine.
At a window,

looking down at the church, like a bride I once was.
The city is full of guests who dance at the edge of 'yes'

eager to know how life can fit in a word,
how to trust this turning world.

I imagine their lips bleeding when asking.
Today, I prefer no answers,

only willing to feel
the thunderous mechanics of waves in the air.

A long look through the window.
The wait for the bells to strike back.

And tomorrow, when the clock says it is time,
it's just a day when the bells sway.

Tolling. Telling.
Louder. Heavier. Closer.

At the River

Another river, today, reminded me.
A tremble of light in a drop
of rain. A baby snake
on pebbles, a proem to our
new summer. Boys
collecting glassy stones,
shiny miracles to be thrown away.
My mother's voice, echoing,
Don't go down to the river!

I went in deep,
looked into your river-green eyes
soaring over the rocks,
the wildlife thirsty for you,
the cold-blooded quietly
buried in their bed.
A swift current of fear
rippled through me,
as if you were playing.
Or claiming.

Once, in front of you,
I took off my dress,
imagined swimming
down to your river mouth.

The tributaries bore us—toward
a lake, or a sea.
The years curled with us
in the creeks and the valleys.

It is Christmas again,
an outing in pink glow.

Calm today, you gently part
the fertile land.
The earth moves for you, with you.

Waist deep in your grasp,
a small wave brings me a shiver.
Your perennial urgency for life,
smoothing your heart of stone.

I dive into you until I can't breathe.
You carry me up for air and sunlight.
What was and will be,
you hold now and flow your way.

Once in Paris

We rub the shame off our towels.
What was there, we will try to forget.

Our fingertips will burn
with repetition.

Pretend, pretend.
I am dying,

but I wear my best dress
as if I am not.

Your hands, hold hands
four ivory nets,

underside softness and
warmth that's familiar.

Carelessly spread fingers
caught in rings of flames.

No bed with cushions.
His side. Her side.

A wild waltz that ends
gently with a promise that

the future will bleed and
the past is a stain of highest erosion.

Royal Adelaide Hospital

We cross the grey way.
Enter the room with people

whose faces carry
love and loss as one.

Our bodies inside set traps
to scare us to death.

A doll display of nurses
smile behind our backs.

Up and down the stairs
I am out of breath.

Not enough iron in my blood
to plot a hope, or cheat a death,

I swim in the air sideways
leaving no trace of bad habits

as if it matters now, or
did it ever?

You take my arm and risk
our Mediterranean dream.

This warmth will sink easy
in the murmur of the sea

in waves of conversations around us.
Patients, doctors, families, friends.

We believe we are invincible,
until we find ourselves in a place

like this, coming up for the air
we forgot we needed.

In the car as you drive,
I lean on the window

against this rainy day
looking ahead, then

turning to you,
I could feel

the years behind us
those shooting at us.

The raindrops playing
in my eyes.

How far can we go
and not get anywhere?

Serbian Christmas

At the front door in January
the oak branch is green.
Acorns, wheat, and lollies
thrown above our heads.

'Can I light the candle, Mum?'
'No.' *You are a girl—*
I almost repeat
my mother's words.

A canvas of stitched yarn
hung like hope
above the solemn occasion.
Inside, the chairs are arranged.

We peel cutlery off the table
meat off the bone
crosscut the bread
prepared with love.

A candle burns in the glass of salt
dissolving our faces till midnight
then
we sing for the motherland
and cry in our sleep like babies.

This Morning, a Fresh Beginning

Coffee and warm milk
suppress the appetite for secrets.

A bittersweet takeaway.
A sprinkle of a promise

that there are no promises
although, it is Thursday

and there will be other
days with a similar name

or time that's not right,
but almost.

This winter morning
take a step back

to the doorstep dust
garnished with sunshine.

This day will rise
like a warm bread

in hand-made heat
the home-grown flavour

of a suitable life.

Letting Go in Istanbul

I lean into the Bosphorus to see Istanbul
lying on two continents, falling asleep on neither.
A wave slightly lifts the boat and drops it.
Half a glass of wine begins to taste like weakness
and everything inside it
is divided into the even sips of
if and *only*.
Where do you go when you close your eyes?
Not so close to the edge, I gaze into the night.
A body remembers a dive into distance comfortably.
A young man with a camera gestures me to pose,
shows me how to lift my glass and smile for a small fee.
His eyes are lined with charcoal.
He takes a photo with the bridge behind me,
it feels familiar, this strength from afar
the bridge hanging in the dark,
in perfect harmony with sky and water,
holding hands with the city,
saying come closer, in front of everyone
without words or movement,
yet any closer and I worry
that behind me is always a bridge
I burn as I cross,
accidently, completely.

My eyes caress its greatness
weighing elegance and exhaustion
in a sign of a scale,
uniting and pulling apart
my memories of those
who never held hands,
or not anymore,
then the hands of my husband
and my children who always let go so easily
to run with excitement toward others.

In a moment another woman
tosses her hair playfully for a photo.
Much has been said and not meant.
No time left for regrets.

The boat turns back on a gentle wave,
lights breaking on the water
between continents. All this weight
tenderly sparkles towards midnight.

Dying Art of Bargaining

1.
It is the city with many names,
all of them true.

Istanbul is a personal choice.
The relics are buried.

Be curious about the ceilings.
Make a point about pointlessness.

Gabriel is an angel.
An angel is not a saint.

2.
Want to trust this world,
but negotiate the price?

3.
The marble jar full of gold
is now full of lemonade.
A sweet death.

4.
The ceiling makes me giddy.
If Gabriel claps his wings ...

5.
Here the walls meet.
The wall from the 4th century
meets the wall from the 14th century.
They continue to be walls.
Sacred and damaged.

Blame the people,
an old conqueror,
the earthquakes and storms.

6.
A tired-looking tourist looks up
for the built-in prophecies.
A heart surgeon worries for the heart of civilisation.
A waiter is too young for the language of demand.

7.
A poem is a smothered detonation.
Here a lover is yet to be executed.

I return to the news of stabbing.

8.
I know this story backwards.
It ends with *what were you thinking?*

9.
Once a newly painted picture
is now a dark place.

10.
We forget what we've demolished or built.
A dog needs to be fed.

11.
There is nothing mean about bridges.

12.
Where do you go when you close your eyes?
Not so close to the edge.

13.
The world ahead is not yet glued.

14.
Birds fly in and out.
Around the corner
street musicians play their final tune.
I look obsessively at the ceilings.

15.
Things we position up high
always look down on us.

16.
The picture. The writing.
This story. No end to it.

17.
I look at the sky.
It looks creased.

Love doesn't die.
It shapeshifts.

Like hair.
I cut the curly ends.

18.
An omelette with veggies, but no eggs?
The waiter worries about the order of things.

19.
In Türkiye, I am from Australia,
unfolding a perfectly folded scarf.

A shop assistant offers
tea in a tulip-shaped glass,

reviving the dying art of bargaining.
He heard about Australians from his customers.

He confirms the news:
people work, don't smile.

I feel a slide down the silky side of the world,
and I am holding onto its threads.

20.
The shop assistant climbs
through a few English words toward his village,

to show me the stone
where the plain truth lies above the men lost in wars.

Their wives weave their love into scarves.
The scarves are worth the price.

But wives in Australia? They just go places.
Or call a gardener when the leaves fall from trees.

I fold a scarf back like a thought of spring in Australia,
the daises my father poisoned instead of weeds,

a leaf that shakes in the wind.
Falls in its own time.

And here I am, alone in Istanbul,
remembering to smile,

saying thank you for the tea.

Garden of Stones

Aleksinac in August

1.
The first place I go
after I find the house key under the pot
and unlock the door.
My hand reaches for the switch on the wall
through the cobwebs.
The new neighbour across the road waved today,
he is glad to see the lights are on.
Our windows are open. The night curtain shifts
with air. I hide behind it to undress.
Only the street cats are missing. Their many lives
have gone gently into a distant dream.
I walk toward the bed with lightness,
worshipping my previous life.

2.
A pear falls off the tree.
A familiar thud on dry ground.
I feel it deep in my womb.
At sunrise, the woodpecker is back.
Might not be the same one.
I am not who I once was, either.
His drumming into the trunk echoes.

His tree pocket suggests he flies solo.
It takes a long time to grow strong wings.
The morning slowly invites other birds.
I pack for the cemetery:
candles, matches, brandy and biscuits.

3.
On the way, the neighbours say I brought the rain
but it always rains when I walk toward the dead.
There are holes on the road.
I walk as if looking for what I left behind.
At the gate, the keeper talks with his fist
When you find it, hold it tight.
But he thinks of things that are yet to be born,
like love and hope.
He says he recognises my walk,
my step over the cobblestones,
the sound of it, like a heartbeat.
I step back, to hear it better.
What is in the centre of a stone, but stone?
When thrown away
it doesn't break the Earth's heart.

4.

The Earth has taken enough,

its face distorted after the storms.

The years of unsaid goodbyes are not coming back.

The stone garden has grown.

Flowers are growing toward it.

Where do I go? He says,

Ahead, after this lifetime,

it will be easier. Then,

we will talk again.

Two crows splash laughter

across the freshly washed sky.

When I step through the gate,

their laugh is perhaps a scream.

I am less cautious in my travels.

I watch one of them closely.

The bearer of warnings is of no use.

Dear crow, no picking at old scabs.

I heal slowly.

Perhaps, *I* should warn *you*.

If I were a crow, I would land next to you.

Smooth my feathers against your life.

What is a greater warning,

being close, or flying high?

I won't try to understand.

5.
It is windy and hot.
The granite dust is sticky on my skin.
The dear ones' stones stand up to the living ones' hearts.
Behind the stones, cats appear.
Unafraid, they seek their owners.
I feed them biscuits.
A sprinkle of brandy onto the ground
then a sip for my soul. A need to clear the air.
A red plastic rose has turned grey.
A reminder to return.
Looking down is not easy.
I kneel to light a candle shielded from the wind.
The sun threatens to burn us all. It doesn't.
Just a light touch on my shoulder. A kiss.

Bridge of Sighs

Karrawirra Parri, 2025

1.
Once upon a time,
there was a small footbridge across the Torrens,
snuggled in a time-worn catchment
of green canopies and cloudbursts.
I found my way there and lost it on the best of days.
It was a narrow crossing to the other side
—almost reckless.
A feeling of lightness in the wind blowing in both directions.
as if winter was still yearning for a choice it never made.

2.
Today, new spring ravishes
the scenery with sweetness.
It's a gift of bliss, gums' silky
sway in the air.
The hair on my arms shivers
like feathers
as birds take flight.
An urge to look up, to know.

3.
There is a lifetime between us. Sometimes nothing.
The years we let loose are invisible to the naked eye.

I tell myself a story about the Mediterranean.
You try to wrap your head around it.

Two pigeons fall from their trees, entangled in desire.
Their dance sets the bridge alight.

They fly away. You smile.
If I blinked, I would've missed it.

4.
In the river, on a long dead log
a cormorant stands,
as still as a portrait,

as thrilling as bad luck
that might swallow us any moment.

Everything around us is muted green.
A paradise, into which we dive as if it were true.

Now and then, coming up for air,
thrilled to be alive, calling it love.

5.
My breath quickens. I try not to tear apart
this ordinary spring day, out of fear of who I am.
A grand illusion. A body half present.
                    A mind half-eaten by doubt.
The river is cold and thin—crowd pleasing.
In its slow soft flow, all my faces disappear
like soldiers weary of fighting.
I peek through my fingers to find
the fraction of the world that lifts me,
gently lets me down.

6.
The pulse of spring above the river,
moves me, swiftly and slowly
                    a leaf is dancing with a breeze,
                    surrendering completely.

A turtle basks still upon a log,
a cat moves like a snake in the grass—

through the lush green. I only see parts of it.
Believe all of it.

7.
There is no river that leads to forever,
but everything is sliding towards it, just the same.

8.
Brown ducks dive and hide their turquoise feathers
like the crown jewels of fallen royalty.

Then catfish, never thinking about being caught in the net.
Their underwater love-play leaves me gasping for air.

9.
A couple stands within a touch.
He leans over her, she tiptoes closer,
as if the sun had placed a guiding hand
of warmth on each back.
At these thrilling heights,
it's best to cross quietly,
or go back quickly.
But here they remain,
on the bridge
halfway falling, halfway flying.
They hold each other tight,
endlessly kiss, kiss, kiss.

Gumnuts

My birthday comes in autumn now, in the golden weather.
The sun has come out of hiding, and I lie happy under
a eucalypt tree. The leaves are glowing, flammable. Between
their naked double-edged blades the gumnuts sway, like
unwrapped gifts, or wooden bells, empty-headed, open
to the light. They appeared suddenly, in small bursts
of tenderness, birthday kisses falling through the branches
onto my hair, my face, scraping down my neck, seeking
a perfect spot to hang. I wore one as might a tree,
a birthmark, a lucky pendant.
The future seemed shinier than a flowering bullet.
I felt tree roots untangling my wishes.
The red earth's lips sucking my life softly.
And I knew that I would lie here a bit longer, widespread
among the leafy blades, with my eucalypt green eyes
taking all in. Fallen gumnuts, the empty eye sockets
that have seen everything and nothing since the first wildfire.

Acknowledgments

Writing and reading go hand in hand, and I often find myself torn between the West and East in style and themes. I return again and again to my literary favourites—Vasko Popa, Anna Akhmatova, Charles Simic—then, the esteemed Australian writers whose insight often surpasses my own understanding of this collection. A heartfelt thank you to Peter Goldsworthy—years ago, discovering your poetry in the waiting room of your surgery was the spark that inspired me to put pen to paper and begin to write. To Kate Llewellyn AO, for the joy and wisdom of your literary guidance and lessons in planting seeds. I have been incredibly fortunate to be part of Kate's legendary tradition of soirees, and to discuss literary works with a brilliant group of women! To Mike Ladd—a poem a month was one poet's commitment for another to grow.

To Jennifer Rutherford and Brian Castro—your support has been a real gift, and I'm so grateful for it.

Thank you to Ken Bolton, Jill Jones and Thom Sullivan for their great suggestions with the line breaks, the rhythm and the sequence.

In 2023, my dear friend and fellow poet Alison Flett passed away, but her voice still echoes between the pages of my early drafts.

To the Metropole Poetry Group in the Blue Mountains, for their generous feedback, poetry exercises, hiking and shared dinners, especially to Mike Ladd, Dael Allison, and Carol Jenkins.

A special thanks to the wonderful John Watson for his incredible poems, advice and letters.

I often found myself immersed in Ted Hughes' *Birthday Letters* delighting in his poetic complexities, which in turn helped me channel my own creative thoughts into poems 'The River', 'The Box of Chocolates' and 'Gifts'.

The line 'their mouths beaten' in 'The Telling of the Bells' might have originated from one of the online articles about bells I could never find again.

The lines 'hoping/to light a way home' in the poem 'On a Street Corner' echo Charles Simic's poem 'The Last Picnic'.

'The Jetty' is a response Kate Llewellyn's poem under the same title in her poetry collection *Harbour*.

'Us and Other Guests' would not exist without Jacqui Boylan's invitation to reflect on our culturally responsive work in Education. Originally written as a vision statement for our team, it was inspired by the life experiences of the Community Liaison Officers—honoured to work alongside you! I'm deeply grateful to the incredible women—Sarah Anstey, Jacqui Boylan, Becc Clark, Sarah Gleed, Tanya Russo, Claire Simmons, and many others who work tirelessly to make a difference in education and create culturally safe spaces for all.

It has been a great pleasure to collaborate with my editor Julia Beaven and the team at Wakefield Press, to whom I am profoundly grateful for their ongoing support.

And finally, to my family—my guiding stars—thank you for your unwavering love.

Wakefield Press is an independent publishing and
distribution company based in Adelaide, South Australia.
We love good stories and publish beautiful books.
To see our full range of books, please visit our website at
www.wakefieldpress.com.au
where all titles are available for purchase.
To keep up with our latest releases and news,
subscribe to the *Wakefield Weekly* at
https://mailchi.mp/wakefieldpress/subscribe

Find us!

Facebook: www.facebook.com/wakefield.press
Instagram: www.instagram.com/wakefieldpress

www.ingramcontent.com/pod-product-compliance
Lightning Source LLC
Chambersburg PA
CBHW031422160426
43196CB00008B/1016